Psychology and Health Series:

Volume 4

BODY IMAGE

HOW WE SEE OURSELVES AND OTHERS; HOW THIS CAN LEAD TO PROBLEMS.

Marios Savva

I dedicate all my books in my Psychology and Health series, to my loving family.

TABLE OF CONTENTS

THE AUTHOR

As an experienced psychologist currently living in Birmingham, England, and a member of the British Psychological Society, I now have the fervent desire to start writing books on psychology for people to read. I have endeavoured to make my books interesting to read and, with a little humour, as some psychology material can get 'heavy' and slightly complicated. BODY IMAGE: *HOW WE SEE OURSELVES AND OTHERS; HOW THIS CAN LEAD TO PROBLEMS*, is the fourth book in the Psychology and Health series. Readers can contact me on: marios.spurs@hotmail.co.uk.

Other books by the author

Stress

Depression

Know Thyself

Drugs and Addictions

I Want To Sleep

Introduction

We all care to a varying degree about our body image, how we see ourselves, and about how others see us. For a lot of people around the world, especially in Western societies, this concern reaches a point that a lot of times can affect our psychology negatively, and our way of living. In extreme cases, which unfortunately is becoming more and more common, this concern becomes an intense worry, and worse still, can develop in to a psychological disorder.

This book focuses on the critical aspects of stress, anxiety and the media on young adolescent men's and women's body image. We shall attempt to better understand the concepts presented and explained, and furthermore, illustrate the significance of the media's influence on adolescent women's judgements of their own schema and body image.

Despite the substantial amount of controversy that exists surrounding the precise effects media has on people in every psychosocial aspect, it is an indisputable fact that the media acts as a powerful mediator of human judgement. Some researchers hypothesize that the media is often seen by people as the easiest way to place a responsibility upon and pass judgement without realizing that other factors are actually the true cause. Other researchers believe that the media does in fact influence peoples' lives in a variety of ways and patterns, such as how to think, act, and look.

People can detect the sway the media has on vital aspects of modern civilization. A concerned individual has no option but to get informed about politics through newspapers and television and this gives him/her the illusion of choice. A mother is virtually being "taunted" by an advertisement on the grounds that she is not paying close attention to what she feeds her baby and should switch to a better product. A teenage girl is obliged to conform to the dress code among her peers to be socially accepted; it is imperative for her to copy the fashion preferences she can scavenge from beauty and fashion magazines. It goes without saying that all these statements have face validity, and one could quite easily notice these patterns in any western civilized country.

Specifically, concerning body image, a question that usually arises is: "What facilitates the acceptance of one's body image and their appearance self-schema?"

As we shall see in this book, two of the most crucial facilitators are stress and anxiety, which often manifest into disorders, and, of course, the media itself.

The Psychological Concept of Beauty

There is an old adage that states that beauty is in the eye of the beholder. Individuals observe a variety of looks they think are beautiful. The psychological concept of beauty (in people) is one of the things to be aware of in today's world. It is well known that many people prefer a long, thin aquiline nose. Some people prefer tats on a person where others don't. Where did the psychological concepts of beauty come from and how do they manifest in our ideas of what we consider to be beautiful?

Although some concepts of beauty are almost universally accepted, one theory supports that the concept of beauty has to do with parents. Many times, as theory supports, people wish to find beauty ideals that are similar to what we experienced growing up. It is true that from a psychological perspective Freudian or psychological experiences of beauty are scarce. The Psychoanalysis theory on this matter, compares our concepts of beauty often-times from what we observed in our parents.

However, it is no secret that beauty of symmetry or proportions is something that has been long regarded as beautiful; psychological tests have borne this out. Many people are considered to be beautiful when they have features that may be considered to be baby faced or soft in feature.

Proportion size is also fundamental to our beauty concepts. Take for instance the proportion of individuals that were in Victorian England. Tiny waists were some of the things that were considered to be very attractive. Smooth and modern features were considered to be beautiful. Perfectly shaped proportions and sharp features are very beautiful to some people. Curvy hips and shapely proportions are the items that most people find attractive in women rather than straight angles. This applies to beauty for women, as most men are looking for fertile females and the curvy lower portions indicate fertility.

Beauty is a holistic standard psychologically. This refers to the sum of the parts instead of each part being taken individually. This is the concept of viewing beauty holistically, and the way that it is often done. It is safe to say that there are many aspects of beauty that individuals look for and the characteristics are quite subjective in nature. Men who have athletic or muscular bodies are more attractive to women and a number of studies bear this out. As we know however, since beauty is subjective, in individuals it stands to reason that many men may not prefer curvy or curvaceous women. Many women also may not prefer muscle bound men.

There are many traits and looks that people consider to be attractive, however, this is not across the board or in every situation. Again, beauty is subjective and in the eye of the beholder, that is why universal standards of beauty are elusive and something that individuals can not necessarily quantify or may with an iron clad rule out. People are different psychologically, and it stands to reason that their ideas of what is beautiful is also different. In terms of psychological aspects of beauty, it is still largely subjective with different cultures and individuals giving their ideas about what makes someone beautiful in their particular estimation.

The psychology of beauty has long been a concept that has fascinated psychologists and researchers across the ages. What and how beauty is determined are some of the fundamental concepts to consider when looking at the factors that determine the concept of beauty and what makes up beauty - psychologically speaking. Is there a fundamental concept that is worldwide that determines beauty or is it simply subjective? Obviously, anthropologically speaking, beauty differs from culture to culture. These are just some of the ways that this issue functions in real life.

The one fundamental concept in the concept of beauty that seems to be the same from culture to culture is the idea of symmetry or proportion of features. This seems to be something that is also recognized in the animal kingdom as animals tend to prefer those who are symmetrical in proportion. Some of the other aspects that seem to indicate beauty in other people seems to be an aspect of the facial structure.

In psychological experiments, individuals always pick as more beautiful faces where the forehead and jawbones are aligned. This bears out the entire symmetry in the features argument. It is seen as desirable and preferable when there are no issues with bones being longer or more prominent than others. This is the way that individuals recognize what they the wish to see in faces that they like. Many people will use the concepts of beauty to pick a mate or to determine who gets the job promotion.

It is interesting that individuals across the continents while they differ in their concepts of beauty still find it something that they are looking for when they are looking for beautiful people and faces. It is simply one of the things that individuals do agree on in this fundamentally subjective concept; symmetry and alignment. There is also the concept of advertising in beauty. How much is natural preference like the hourglass figure for instance, and how much beauty is a function of advertising is something that needs to be looked at and discussed. Beyond symmetry, those in Western culture seem to prefer those who have a small jaw and large eyes. Chinese men prefer those with small feet while some African cultures prefer those with large discs in their lips. Psychologically speaking, although beauty may be a subjective concept, it is also what you are used to – what you learnt constituted beauty when growing up in a certain culture.

There are other things to think of when considering the aspects of beauty. In society as a whole, people considered to be attractive frequently have higher levels of intelligence are better adjusted and more successful than their less attractive peers. Psychologically, people are more likely to attribute positive attributes to people who are considered to be more attractive. Look at the concept of the good witch and the bad witch for instance. The good witch has only positive attributes for instance, and is quite comely, whereas the bad witch is unattractive, and has unattractive features, warts and other unsavoury aspects of her looks. Many people fall into these traps and can play a factor in hiring and choosing friends. There is no doubt that our psychology forms our idea of what or who is beautiful.

Media and Beauty

The media plays an important role in promoting and reflecting the current mainstream culture's standards for ideal beauty, particularly for women. It is very easy to spot how much beauty is overemphasized in the Western societies; TV shows, advertisements, fashion magazines, fitness and beauty products, cosmetics, and more. Although there are no perfect criteria that people can use to judge their own or another's attractiveness, a worldwide standard of beauty was made possible by the rise of mass media, and by showing attractive models, they raised the standards of attractiveness. Beauty industries and fashion business, such as cosmetics, diet foods, plastic surgery, have expanded their economic investments and emphasized the need for appearance-enhancing products and behaviours. Among the various media, much attention has been given to the advertising industry for their negative influence on women because advertised models are nearly perfect in their body shape and size as well as their physical attractiveness.

There is evidence that shows that advertising is a major contributor to eating disorders with one finding stating that advertising is a $130 billion industry and the most powerful educational force in America. The fashion and beauty industries appeal to female consumers to use their products by presenting attractive images (e.g. young, slim, and attractive models with flawless skin) through advertisement.

It is important to place emphasis on the way people process information under different psychological states. As we shall see later on, the media is an important variable concerning the way individuals learn to perceive and feel about their physical appearance. All agents of the media today keep bombarding us, through various means with messages on how our bodies should look like, and generally a set of rules and norms on how we should look, behave, etc. There is increasing research on how people process and accept these media messages.

Several researchers have examined the effects of mood on message processing and elaboration. Research findings in this area are complex and sparse. Some research findings suggest that bad mood (including low-anxiety) leads to greater message processing and heightened elaboration as compared to a good or a neutral mood. However, some studies have shown that high anxiety reduces cognitive capacities and diminishes elaboration and recall, compared to low or neutral anxiety. In addition, other studies have demonstrated that very sad people were less likely to process and elaborate adequately than happy people, due to their psychological breakdown caused by depression. Finally, some recent research has illustrated that people in a happy mood tend to process more effectively a message (especially a non-threatening one), compared with people in a bad mood.

Body Dissatisfaction and Eating Disorders

Today, at least 2 million female Americans have a clinically relevant eating disorder. The scientific literature in this area has reported that men are much less likely than women to suffer from clinical eating disorders such as anorexia or bulimia nervosa. Eating disorders have become the third most common form of chronic illness among adolescent women aged 15 to 19 years and approximately 90% to 95% of individuals who go for treatment are female. Adolescent women are four times more likely to develop an eating disorder than are adolescent men, compared with women in the general population who are 10 times more likely to be diagnosed with eating disorders than are men.

Anorexia Nervosa is a relatively rare disorder among adolescents aged 10 to 24, especially men; however, the prevalence has increased among adolescents aged 15 to 19 years since 1935. Cases of eating disorders have been observed in males as well. For example, the so-called Adonis complex is associated with something similar to Body Dysmorphic Disorder, where young men strive to achieve the ideal image of the perfect body by over-exercising, dieting, and by using steroids to achieve a thin and muscular body. Data from studies of adult men diagnosed with eating disorders indicated that the onset (when it first begins) tends to occur at a later age than for women and that they have a higher prevalence of pre-morbid obesity, and that they are less concerned with weight maintenance.

Generally, if we exclude the differences between the two genders, we can say that body image dissatisfaction is acknowledged as an extensive problem experienced by a large proportion of society. In simple words, we can say that body image is how we feel and think about our physical appearance. It is the mental image of one's body, and simply refers to how individuals perceive their own bodies. Moreover, it has to do and with personal evaluations (e.g.

body satisfaction-dissatisfaction) and associated emotions concerning physical attributes, as well as investment in appearance, for example, the importance someone places on his or her own appearance.

Many researchers have found that body image or body satisfaction is positively related to self-esteem, and that lower self-esteem, on the other hand, was associated with abnormal eating behaviour. Because a positive relationship exists between body image and self-esteem, it is reasonable to expect that a poor and distorted body image would be associated with other indicators of poor psychological health along with low self-esteem. Remember, body image distortion is defined as the inaccurate subjective perception of one's body or body part. So, in other words, a poor or distorted body image is an important risk factor for the development of an eating disorder. Additionally, low self-esteem has been found to be related to depressive symptomatology, mostly in women.

The more dissatisfied a woman is with her body, the more likely she will engage in drastic means to lose weight (e.g. restricting food or purging). Moreover, research has found strong associations between body dissatisfaction and eating disorders. In one study, women were shown attractive images from magazines and found that the exposure produced "negative affective states" (depression, shame, guilt, anger, insecurity), which predicted (indicated the future probability) for bulimic tendencies. Research also has demonstrated that perfection (especially a maladaptive one) is one of many psychological factors contributing to the development of either anorexia or bulimia. In addition to perfectionism, other factors contributing to eating disorders are a distorted, fragile and negative sense of self and a sense of powerlessness.

Individuals who are prone and predisposed to developing an eating disorder are; more likely to be influenced by negative social evaluations, they are less likely to have a strong sense of self and identity, they are more likely to have low self esteem, and they are more vulnerable to stress and less capable of adapting to and handling stressful situations.

Socio-Cultural Issues

As with everything in psychology, we have to consider factors such as culture and social norms when investigating human behaviour and psychological disorders. It is clear from large amounts of evidence that concepts such as beauty, body image, eating habits, and dieting, are significantly influenced by culture and the power of social norms; what is expected, what seems right and wrong and what is presented by the media as the ideal.

For example, several researchers found evidence that obesity in women diagnosed with eating disorders may not be a function of their being female but may be significantly affected by the complex transitions of the 'female role' in culture. Some psychologists infer also concerning this issue, that individuals are actively involved in constructing their own social identity, and many scholars have examined how everyday symbolic forms like media and technology shape behaviour. The *thin ideal* is transmitted and reinforced via a number of different socio-cultural mechanisms, primarily parents, peers and the media.

By observing socio-cultural attitudes, it is not surprising that from early childhood, girls learn from various agents of socialization that appearance is especially important to them as girls and that they should be concerned with it. In addition, from their families, young girls learn that one of their important functions is to be pretty. Girls appear to internalize readily these societal messages on the importance of pursuing attractiveness.

The socio-cultural influences thought to contribute to eating disorders include the thin ideal body image for women, and in constructing the female gender role, and also the great importance of appearance for women's societal success. The mass media and children's books also teach girls about the importance of appearance. A survey called "Women on words and Images" (1972) revealed again that girls from a young age were constantly concerned about how they look, whereas boys never were. Developmental studies have documented that girls are more concerned than boys about looking attractive. Parents, teachers, and peers all describe girls as more focused than boys on their looks, and also boys tend to choose toys involving physical and mechanical activity, whereas girls select toys related to aesthetic beauty and nurture.

Thus, women who are at a great risk for bulimia for example, are those who have accepted and internalized more deeply the socio-cultural norms about thinness and attractiveness. In other words, the more a woman believes that "what is fat is bad, what is thin is beautiful, and what is beautiful is good," the more she will work toward thinness and be distressed about fatness. A complex relationship exists between ethno-cultural identity and eating behaviours. This interaction combines nationality, ethnicity, culture, and social status and sometimes this interaction results in the development of unusual eating patterns among those who are attempting to adjust to the world around them. Psychologists who have examined these issues have found that regardless of the ethnic group status, most individuals are subject to the standards of the dominant culture, particularly when their culture or racial/ethnic group of origin is devalued by the dominant culture. Under these conditions, cultural and ethnic identity, social, and individual factors contribute to determine whether disordered eating symptomatology occurs.

Data on the relationship between homosexuality and eating disorders comes from studies with adult gays and lesbians. However, there is no conclusive evidence concerning this issue and very little is known about the incidence and prevalence of eating disorders among adolescents who are gay or lesbians, and the overall relationship between eating disorders and homosexuality remains unclear.

Historical & Cultural Differences Concerning Eating Disorders

In general, researchers believed only Caucasian, upper middle-class women who lived in industrialized or Western countries developed eating disorders. A growing body of evidence suggests that black women are less vulnerable to body-image dissatisfaction and are more proud of their bodies than Anglo-Americans and Hispanics. Studies show that Blacks are less concerned about weight than Whites, exhibit fewer weight-reduction behaviours, such as dieting and exercising, and have lower incidences of eating disorders than Whites.

The historical exclusion of minorities, men, and people from non-western or non-industrialized countries as research participants was based on an original observation that anorexia nervosa was more commonly found in wealthier classes of society than among labourers or lower classes. Current research supports this conclusion for Anorexia Nervosa, but not for bulimia nervosa or binge-eating disorders. Women of colour around the world and male athletes are increasingly being diagnosed with Binge-Eating Disorder and Bulimia Nervosa.

Traditionally, detection of these symptoms is underestimated because of the belief that eating disorders do not exist among people of colour, and because of the social stereotypes that being chubby or obese is "normal" for African, Hispanic, Native, and Asian Americans. When these individuals present themselves for evaluation or therapy, most clinicians do not even examine issues around food and body image as potential sources of mental problems. Eating disorders do exist among women in South Asia but may be related to what is known as "personal agency", for example, some women may starve themselves as a means of having a sense of *some* control over their lives. Detection may also be a problem for Japanese-American women, specifically because the stereotype of "thinness" may be an obstacle that prevents clinicians from exploring the presence of eating disorders in this population. Several studies supported the notion that a separation from one's culture correlates with eating disorder symptoms such as self-starvation or binge-eating among people of colour.

In Western or industrialized countries, being overweight or obese has negative consequences and may result in biases. Those biases can affect everything; hiring and promotion, peer relationships, dating opportunities, self-esteem, eating practices, and dieting. In Western cultures and in the United States in particular, thinness is associated with attractiveness, fitness, and health, whereas obesity is associated with poor health, lack of will and self-control, and unattractiveness. Female adolescents in particular are more likely to be affected and influenced by other women's views of attractiveness.

Anorexia and related eating disorders are rare in non-Western cultures. One theory regarding the lower incidence of eating disorders among women in Asia (China, India, and Japan) and other non-Western countries is that these groups have a greater acceptance of higher body weights. Slimness or being thin is not considered important for attractiveness, and fatness is accepted more easily and even encouraged among some groups and cultures in the non-Western world.

Fatness may be considered as a sign of beauty in some non-Western cultures. Moreover, it is more accepted in these countries but not necessarily valued or respected. Nowadays, the blending of what constitutes beauty across different socio-economic levels, different cultures, different races, and different ethnic groups may make plumpness or chubbiness less desirable in all regions of the world. Women of higher socio-economic status are more likely to be preoccupied with beauty and fashion and exhibit higher concerns about their body.

Obesity traditionally has been least punished and criticized in the lower socio-economic classes. Interestingly, there also appears to be a relationship between certain types of eating behaviour and femininity. In one study, women who were described as eating small meals were rated significantly more feminine, less masculine, and more attractive than women who ate large meals, whereas for men, the meal size didn't have an effect on the ratings. Another study suggested that women may actually restrict their food intake in the service of making a favourable impression on men.

We can thus see that concepts such as femininity, beauty, obesity, thinness, are importantly influenced by an individual's cultural standards and norms, but we can see at the same time that the mixing of ethnicities, races and cultures worldwide, combined with the powerful and uncontrollable insertion of media messages, set the standard of beauty of the Westernised model and gradually, the beauty of fatness or chubbiness that is accepted in some cultures will eventually be eliminated.

Anorexia Nervosa

Obesity and dieting are common among the young generation. In a 1998 study of adolescents, 66% of women and 20% of men reported they had tried to lose weight during the 30 days prior to the study. In a large study of adolescent girls, it was found that the pressure to be thin (the thin-ideal internalization), body dissatisfaction, and binge eating were positively correlated with dieting, and that binge eating predicted increased dieting. Other researchers supported these factors, but they also suggested that dieting may be a response to bulimic pathology.

In general, eating disorders are characterized by severe disturbances in eating behaviour. Let's recall the two most well known types of eating disorders; Anorexia Nervosa and Bulimia. Anorexia Nervosa is characterized by a refusal to keep even the minimally accepted normal body weight. There is an intense fear of gaining weight and a significant disturbance in the perception of body size and shape. In one criterion, the individual maintains a body weight that is below a minimally normal level for age and height. Specifically, the individual weighs less than 85% of that weight that is considered normal for that person's age and height or fails to make the expected weight gain during a period of growth, leading to body weight less than 85% of that which was expected. A clinician treating someone with this disorder, in determining a minimally normal weight, should not only consider the medical guidelines concerning the relationship between an individual's height and weight, but also the individual's body build and body history.

Usually, weight loss is accomplished primarily through reduction in total food intake. Although individuals may begin by excluding from their diet those things which they perceive to be high in calories, they end up by restricting their diet to only a few specific foods. Additional methods of weight loss include purging (i.e. self induced vomiting or the misuse of laxatives or diuretics) and/or excessive exercise. In diagnosing Anorexia Nervosa, the individual has an intense fear of gaining weight which doesn't seem to go away even when the person continues to lose weight. In another criterion, the image and perception about body and shape is significantly distorted or there is a significant denial of the seriousness of the current low body weight. Some individuals feel totally overweight while others realize that although they are thin, they still look obsessively for body parts (i.e. abdomen, buttocks, thighs) that might have the slightest amount of fat and they repeatedly check and measure their exact body weight.

Additionally, in many instances in women, there are symptoms of amenorrhoea, which is the absence of at least three consecutive menstrual cycles. According to the International Classification of Diseases (ICD-10), Anorexia Nervosa is diagnosed when A) body weight is less than 85% of the normal weight for that age (body mass index is 17.5 or less). B) Weight loss self-induced by the avoidance of "fattening foods" (self-induced vomiting or purging or excessive exercise or the use of appetite suppressants or diuretics). C) Psychopathological dread of fatness; persistent, intrusive, overvalued ideal and a self-imposed low-weight threshold. D) In post-menarcheal women, amenorrhoea (the absence of at least three consecutive menstrual cycles). E) Amenorrhoea (women) and loss of sexual interest and potency (men) may have elevated levels of growth hormone or cortisol, changes in the peripheral metabolism of the thyroid hormone, and abnormalities of insulin secretion.

The self-esteem of individuals with Anorexia Nervosa is highly dependent on their body shape and weight. Weight loss is viewed as an impressive achievement and a sense of self-control and self-discipline whereas weight gain is perceived as an unacceptable loss of self-control. It is important to point out also that though some individuals realize that they are thin, they deny the serious consequences that are caused by their malnutrition. The individual is often brought to a professional by a family member after severe weight loss has occurred (or failure to make expected gains). These individuals, most of the time, lack insight and they are in a state of considerable denial about their problem.

The following subtypes (a, b, and c) can be used to specify the presence or absence of regular binge eating or purging in Anorexia Nervosa. The restricting type (a) specifies cases where weight loss is accomplished primarily through dieting and/or excessive exercise. During the current episode (b), these individuals have not regularly engaged in binge eating or purging. The Binge-Eating/purging type (c) is used to specify the individuals who are regularly engaged in binge eating or purging (or both) during the current episode. Most individuals with Anorexia Nervosa who binge eat also purge, though self-induced vomiting or the misuse of diuretics, laxatives, enemas, etc. However, some individuals in this subtype, do not binge eat, but they do often purge after the consumption of small amounts of food.

Individuals with Anorexia Nervosa, when seriously underweight, exhibit depressive symptoms, social withdrawal, irritability, insomnia and diminished interest in sex. Obsessive compulsive symptoms also occur, since people with this disorder are usually involved with intense checking and rechecking of their body shape and weight, estimating caloric intake, uncontrollable thoughts about food, etc. Depressive and obsessive symptoms and a strong family history of affective disorders and alcohol abuse have been found in people with eating disorders. Of course, thoughts about food in many cases occur because the person suffers from extreme starvation. If this is not the case, and the individual suffers from intense, intrusive thoughts that are not related to food, then a diagnosis of obsessive- compulsive disorder is warranted.

Anorexia Nervosa has to be differentiated also from other disorders that might exhibit similar symptoms i.e. Major Depressive Episode, Obsessive-Compulsive Disorder, Social Phobia and Body-Dysmorphic Disorder. There needs to be a differentiation between Anorexia Nervosa and other general medical conditions that might cause significant weight loss (e.g. gastrointestinal disease, brain tumours, AIDS, arterial problems, etc.) In these cases, even though a significant weight loss is observed there are not any psychological underlying reasons behind them like for example, a distorted body image. In Major Depressive Disorder, weight is again reduced but the individual doesn't show any desire for further weight loss or excessive fear of weight gain and generally isn't concerned about body image.

Some of the features of Anorexia Nervosa resemble symptoms of other disorders and in many cases other disorders co-occur with Anorexia Nervosa. For example, individuals with Anorexia might be embarrassed to be seen eating in public, just like with individuals with social phobia. They may be preoccupied with thoughts about food and body shape, just like individuals with Obsessive-Compulsive disorder or they may be preoccupied with a real or imagined defect in bodily appearance as in Body-Dysmorphic disorder.

Many physical symptoms and medical conditions might be caused by Anorexia Nervosa. Extreme starvation and malnutrition might cause severe damage to internal vital organs. Most often there are complaints of constipation, abdominal pain, cold intolerance, lethargy and excess energy. The most obvious finding on physical examination is emaciation (abnormal thinness caused by lack of nutrition or by disease). There might also be significant hypo-tension, hypothermia, dryness or yellowness of skin, hypertrophy of the salivary glands, and individuals who induce vomiting might have dental erosion or scars on the hands from the contact with teeth when using the hand to induce vomiting.

Bulimia Nervosa

Bulimia Nervosa is characterized by episodes of binge eating. An episode of binge eating is characterized by eating in a discrete period of time (e.g. within any 2-hour period) an amount of food that is definitely larger than most people would eat during a similar period of time and under similar circumstances. Also, it is important to state that continual snacking on small amounts of food throughout the day is not considered a binge and a clinician treating someone with this disorder should be very cautious considering the <u>context</u> in which the eating occurred (e.g. what is considered as a normal or excessive meal, if it was a holiday or a celebration at the time, etc.) An episode may be continued in more than just one setting, for example, an individual may begin a binge at a restaurant and then continue it when going home. This cycle of binge eating and subsequent compensatory behaviours typically occur on an average of at least two times a week.

Usually, individuals with this disorder especially crave sweets and high-caloric and rich-carbohydrate foods like ice creams or cakes. However, abnormality exists not in the nutritional substances that these individuals want but in the amount that it is consumed. Individuals with this disorder feel ashamed about their problem, that's why they try to conceal it. Binge eating is mostly triggered by environmental stressors and as a way to cope with states of dysphoria. Sometimes it is also caused by feelings of embarrassment concerning someone's body shape and weight. However, after the temporary relief that these individuals experience after their binge eating, depressive symptoms occur.

There is a sense of a lack of control over eating during the episode (e.g. a feeling that one cannot stop eating or control what or how much one is eating). However, this impairment in control during the binge episode is not always absolute, since many individuals may cease their binge eating when someone interrupts them.

Recurrent inappropriate compensatory behaviour is present in order to prevent weight gain, such as self-induced vomiting; misuse of laxatives, diuretics, enemas or other medications; fasting or excessive exercise. Self-induced vomiting occurs in 80%-90% of individuals with this disorder and approximately one third of individuals with Bulimia Nervosa misuse laxatives after an episode of binge eating. Excessive exercise is also one method used by individuals to prevent weight gain. Exercise is considered excessive when it significantly interferes with social and occupational functioning, when it is performed in unusual times and places and when these individuals insist on exercise even after injuries or other medical complications.

Exaggerated concerns about body shape and gaining weight are similar, to a large extent, to those who suffer from Anorexia Nervosa. The disturbance does not occur exclusively during episodes of Anorexia Nervosa. Anorexia Nervosa also includes concerns about eating in public, feelings of ineffectiveness, a strong need to control one's environment, inflexible thinking, limited emotional expression and social spontaneity. A large amount of people with Anorexia Nervosa also meet the criteria for a Personality Disorder. Furthermore, it is important to note that individuals with the Binge-Eating/Purging Type of Anorexia Nervosa, in comparison with the Restricting type mentioned earlier, are more likely to also have other impulse-control problems, to abuse alcohol or drugs, to be more sexually active, to have more suicidal attempts, and personality disturbances which likely meet the criteria for Borderline Personality Disorder.

There are two Bulimia Nervosa subtypes:

- Purging type: During the current episode of bulimia nervosa, the person has regularly engaged in self-induced vomiting or the misuse of laxatives, diuretics or enemas.

- Non-purging type: During the current episode of bulimia nervosa, the person has used inappropriate compensatory behaviours, such as fasting or excessive exercise, but has not regularly engaged in self-induced vomiting or the misuse of laxatives, diuretics or enemas.

Individuals with Bulimia Nervosa are usually within the normal weight range and it is a little uncommon among obese individuals. Depressive symptoms, anxiety and other mood disorders co-occur usually with Bulimia Nervosa and many individuals attribute their mood disturbances to Bulimia Nervosa. However, sometimes, mood disorders occur **before** the development of Bulimia Nervosa. All these mood disturbances and anxiety disorders usually remit after the effective treatment for Bulimia Nervosa. In addition, a large amount of individuals with this eating disorder also have a Personality Disorder (most frequently Borderline Personality Disorder) and maybe their eating disturbance is one of the consequences and symptoms of their personality disorders.

Many physical and mental disorders may have eating disturbances and share similar traits with Bulimia Nervosa and it is important to differentiate them. For example, in Kleine-Levin syndrome, which is a general medical condition, there is also disturbed eating behaviour but causes are clearly biological and there is not the psychological profile and the cognitive mechanisms that exist in Eating Disorders. As we have mentioned, an eating disorder might appear because an individual might have an underlying character psychopathology behind it. That character and personality disturbance might cause all the other mood and anxiety disorders and also the eating disorder.

In attempting to understand bulimia, it is crucial to examine again (as we do in all psychological disorders) biological and genetic factors. It is important to remember that women are genetically programmed to have a proportionately higher body fat composition than men, a sex difference that appears to take place across all races and cultures, and the differences between the sexes in fatness increases dramatically on average across the life span. One way in which heredity may influence weight is by determining the ways in which food is metabolised.

Individual differences in metabolic rate seem to be of great significance in determining the efficiency of caloric expenditure. Indeed, even individuals similar in age, sex, weight, and activity level can differ significantly from each other in the amount of calories they eat while sustaining similar levels of body weight. It is ordinarily assumed that those women who are genetically programmed to be heavier than the ideal will be at higher risk for bulimia than those women who are naturally thin.

Clinical evidence suggests that a woman who is heavier than her peers may be more likely to develop bulimia. It has also been found in some research that in addition to the genetic predisposition to a specific body weight, a predisposition to an eating disorder may be genetically transmitted.

It is widely recognized that women have a higher incidence of affective (mood) disorders than men. If a predisposition to affective instability increases an individual's risk of bulimia, then it would represent another answer to the questions of both why women rather than men become bulimic, and which women in particular.

Another risk factor - as several family studies have shown - for the development of eating disorders is heredity. Studies have revealed a high incidence rate of affective disorders among first-degree relatives of bulimic patients. Another crucial negative factor is the degree of cohesion found within the family and the quality of family relationships. For example, a critical family environment in which a great deal of communication revolves around weight, or a critical environment that emphasizes and comments extensively on physical appearance and beauty or a distant father-daughter relationship can all be contributing factors.

The Effects of Media Exposure and the 'Appearance Schema' on Women's Self-Esteem

We shall now examine the effects of media images on women's anxiety levels and self-esteem taking into consideration the **Schema Theory**. A **Schema** (plural *schemata* or *schemas*) describes an organized pattern of thought or behaviour that organizes categories of information and the relationships among them. It can also be described as a mental structure of preconceived ideas, a framework representing some aspect of the world, or a system of organizing and perceiving new information. Schemata influence attention and the absorption of new knowledge: people are more likely to notice things that fit into their schema, while re-interpreting contradictions to the schema as *exceptions* or, distorting them to fit.

Schemata have a tendency to remain unchanged, even in the face of contradictory information. Schemata can help in understanding the world and the rapidly changing environment. People can organize new perceptions into schemata quickly as most situations do not require complex thought when using schema, since automatic thought is all that is required.

People use schemata to organize current knowledge and provide a framework for future understanding. Examples of schemata include social schemas, stereotypes, social roles, scripts, worldviews, and archetypes. Children also adopt a series of schemata to understand the world.

Women with a low appearance schema, even though exposed to the media over a long period of time, possess higher rates of self-esteem and lower rates of anxiety than the schematic ones.

Society has the power to alter people's perceptions of the outside world but also their perception of their own selves. People only tread the path marked for them and never come to realize the internalizing procedures that take place inside them when certain societal stimuli initiate their 'bombardment' procedure. Societal pressure and shame can be devastating influences and it can actually reach a point where they can make or break any individual; advertisements, magazines, television and radio programs, all depict the 'ideal' image of how the human form is supposed to look.

While men are also exposed to the male counterpart stimulus, society instils far more pressure on the female form. This has been the only time during the whole history of humanity where people in completely different hemispheres of the planet starve for completely different reasons. While this book does not attempt to measure direct influence of media images on eating disorders, it does point out several risk factors among women that might evolve to that stage.

Women depicted in the media do not convey the average body type of women, glamorising the unrealistic outside beauty in such a way that inhibits judgement for the other aspects and traits in women. Some women are not affected and do feel satisfied with their bodies and how they look. While others are prone to self-enhancing criticisms and are more likely to engage in eating disorders, become hyper-vigilant about their body weight and looks, and generate much higher anxiety, depression, and dissatisfaction levels as well as lower self-esteem and psychological well-being. Women are treated like commodities in the popular media which glorifies beauty thus often reducing the female form to simply a nude form for the male audience, while intellectual women are portrayed as a danger to the system itself.

Taking into consideration the stereotypes that society unleashes upon women, an increasing number of them are becoming more and more dissatisfied about their body image. Body image refers to an individual's thoughts and feelings about their body and physical appearance. The overwhelming evidence of the female gender as a risk factor for the development of an eating disorder emphasizes the socio-cultural aspect of eating disorders. Specifically, industrialized societies place heavy emphasis on beauty as a core aspect of femininity, and the priority goal of women. Moreover, women try to imitate the lives of famous successful women where they combine beauty, success and career. All these portrayals of feminine beauty and success in the media are believed to have an important influential role in this process of developing a social identity and role formation.

Negative body image attitudes and behaviours generated by certain media influences on the individual well-being is, in turn, magnified as a phenomenon, as a social problem engulfing the vast majority of people within a given society. Is the media responsible when women compare themselves with <u>unattainable</u> images and develop negative body image and self-perception? Is the media the undeniable impetus that instils such pressure on women's body image? And should advertising companies stop advertising unrealistic images when marketing their products? All of the above questions are not easy to answer. Not only is the evidence contradictory, but there is also a virtually endless pool of theoretical propositions that need to be analysed.

Body image refers to our attitudes about our own body, particularly its size, shape, and attractiveness. Body image hosts all the personal evaluations (e.g. body satisfaction-dissatisfaction) and is associated with the physical attributes, emotion and appearance of the individual. According to recent findings, <u>appearance self-schema</u> (realization and evaluation of the appearance of an individual) is a significant factor in women's mood and body image, and not simply solely exposure to media images.

Most women do not actually view their own bodies negatively, unless appearance is of crucial importance to them, but research suggests they are not immune to the media's influence either. This research also shows that exposure to media images over time caused women's depression and anxiety to ascend alarmingly. Continuous exposure to that kind of psychological well-being threat can actually reshape someone's behaviour and attitudes.

New Findings

Eating disorders among young women is estimated at 15% of the population, and according to recent findings body image disturbances begin at a young age, with girls constantly wanting to become thinner. Such negative body images are often linked with strict dieting, which is a strong predictor for serious eating disorders. Certain biological traits, psychological characteristics and family dynamics do contribute to the development of eating disorders. A number of studies have consistently identified the socio-cultural emphasis on thinness as the likely primary cause of the development of these disorders.

Furthermore, a recent model of indirect media effects has been studied. This model proposes that people will perceive some influence of communication on people and, in turn, will change their own attitudes and behaviours accordingly. One theory is that reading beauty and fashion magazines will increase the perceived prevalence of the thin ideal in mass media. In addition, girls of ages 5 – 8 years old had the desire to look thinner, as a result of peer and media influences.

According to the schema theory we mentioned earlier, our perceptions of the world mirror an inter-connection between stimulus variables ('what is really out there) and perceiver variables (what perception shows us). When individuals, for example, invest much of their energy in their appearance and actively engage in actions that further that goal, then they are said to be 'appearance schematic' or schematic on appearance. On the contrary, when appearance is not central to an individual, they are said to be appearance 'a-schematic' or a-schematic on appearance. Women who are appearance schematic portray more symptoms of depressive eating disorders, have lower self-esteem and have higher levels of anxiety than the a-schematic ones.

It is this schematic or a-schematic concept that determines whether the media images can have a powerful impact on women's body image. People with well-defined 'appearance self-schemas' are more likely to focus on appearance information than the a-schematic ones. That means that a-schematic people can become exposed to any media image without that stimuli having any effect on them.

Women who have a higher appearance self-schema will exhibit higher rates of anxiety and lower rates of self esteem. Women with lower rates of appearance schema will depict higher rates of self esteem and lower rates of anxiety. Women with high media exposure rates over a long period of time do not necessarily have higher anxiety and lower self esteem unless they are appearance schematic. Women, when exposed to media images, will have higher anxiety rates over a short period of time.

What we Can Conclude

We have mentioned in this book how stress and anxiety can negatively affect us. To what extent depends on our biological make up (including predisposition), our environment, and our cognitive faculties (misinterpretation of stimuli in our environment). We also looked at several aspects around the role of stress and anxiety, and pointed out the importance of these two concepts with regards to our self concept of beauty, our perceived body image and how this stress and anxiety can lead to eating disorders, especially Anorexia Nervosa and Bulimia Nervosa. An extremely worrying sign is that prevalence keeps rising while the age of onset is sharply decreasing, that is, these disorders are appearing in younger and younger ages. Stress and anxiety can be combated and tempered; sometimes we have the innate instincts for this, sometimes we need to learn the ways and means to.

There are many factors to be analysed when trying to investigate psychological disorders. Eating disorders are a multi-dimensional phenomenon; social, ethno-cultural, biological and psychological aspects should be considered. We have also pointed out how the media plays a powerful role, determining to some extent the way culture defines beauty and the way an individual will process and internalize media messages, and how an individual may feel about his or her body image.

However, how an individual will accept and internalize media messages or social norms depends dramatically on his or her personality traits and predispositions as well as influences from parents, peers, etc. So, for example, if an adolescent girl has certain personality traits that make her vulnerable to social criticism, shame or shyness, she will probably exhibit low self-esteem after observing flawless fitness models in magazines or on television and she will probably engage in pathological behaviours to achieve that unrealistic body.

Adolescent girls who suffer from eating disorders are more likely also to suffer from other psychological disorders like depression. For example, for not being thin or "good" enough, a young female can go on to develop obsessive-compulsive disorder (e.g. an uncontrollable need for checking and rechecking one's body in the mirror, measuring weight repeatedly, constantly camouflaging her appearance, unstoppable thoughts about food, etc.) Another psychological ailment that may develop is social phobia (the inability of exposing one's self in front of a large amount of people due to fear of negative evaluation about one's body and physical appearance).

We can safely say that we cannot isolate one factor in favour of another. Nor does just a sole factor or simply a predisposition imply that it will evolve or turn into a disorder. After looking at the latest research concerning the effects of the powerful "media variable" on body image, and examining the correlation between the media and female body image, we can see a strong correlation between these two variables. Finally, we can see how the factors of stress and self-esteem play a vital role in how we see ourselves, especially concerning our body image.

Body image is important to everyone of us. We care about how we see ourselves and, perhaps more importantly for most, how others see us. It is natural for people who do not possess an ideal body, or close to an ideal body, to be anxious and concerned about it. This is normal. What isn't normal, what becomes abnormal, is when we allow this anxiousness and worry to interfere negatively in our normal way of living; our work, social life, family life and how we function personally.

We have mentioned earlier about the negative consequences that are brought about by our intense dissatisfaction about our body image. Eating disorders, depression, personality disorders to name a few, not to mention suicide in extreme cases.

We should point out here that overweight people (and even individuals with a perfectly thin body) who are stressed and 'down' about their appearance should realise that there are ways, especially in these times we live in, to rectify their appearance with perfectly natural and healthy ways. It may take determination, support from family and friends, and of course, hard work, but positive change is attainable.

But even if for whatever reasons, an individual cannot change their appearance to what they perceive as an acceptable and satisfactory level, we **must not** put our lives in jeopardy because of it.

I would just like to say in closing that, even if to yourself, and, as you see it, to most other people, your appearance is unseemly, or even bad, there are some people around you who think you are just right the way you are and wouldn't change a thing.

Afterword

As we have mentioned in the beginning of this book, we all care to a varying degree about our body image, how we see ourselves, and about how others see us. When this concern though becomes an intense worry it can develop in to psychological disorders, especially eating disorders.

The media influences us greatly, especially for females, the beautiful and thin models in magazines and in the TV adverts are the supposed prototypes for the perfect body. For women who are are very concerned about how they look, that is, they place a great deal of importance on this, they are more susceptible to anxiety and stress when coming in to contact with the concept of beauty in the media. The media bombards us continually with messages about how our bodies should look like. Our appearance self-schema is an important factor in influencing how our exposure to the media and its messages affects us.

How we look does *not* define who we are, contrary to what the media would have us believe. Remember, changing how we *think* changes how we feel.

I hope you enjoyed this book.

The Psychology and Health series

Stress: We Can Master It.

Depression and Sadness: Never Lose Hope – Even If You Can't See Any.

Drugs and Addictions: Some Things You Might Know, A lot of Things You Might Not.

Body Image: How We See Ourselves and Others; How This Can Lead to Problems.

Know Thyself: The Eternal Struggle of The Heart and Mind.

I Want to Sleep: Why We Struggle to Sleep – How We Can Remedy It.